The Wonderful World of Music

The Wonderful World of Music

Benjamin Britten
and Imogen Holst

Collages by Ceri Richards

Doubleday and Company, Inc.

Garden City, New York

Contents

Certain words and phrases in this book are followed by the symbol☞. Whenever you see this symbol it means that you can look up the word or phrase in the alphabetical glossary at the end of the book and find more information or a fuller definition of the term.

1   Sound and Rhythm

No one knows how long ago the first music was made. The Stone Age men, who painted pictures on the walls of caves in France and Spain thousands of years before anybody had invented writing, may have sung songs or played tunes on a bone whistle, perhaps to frighten away the evil spirits at the end of a day's hunting. But we shall never know what they sang or played, for tunes cannot be dug up. We can guess that prehistoric men danced and sang, however, because music flourishes among those who are still living a primitive life.

Sound and rhythm existed on the earth's surface millions of years before there were any men to hear them. The waves of the sea are never still: their sounds change from high to low, and their rhythms change from quick to slow.

Many composers have been interested in these sounds, and have tried to write sea music. What they have written has seldom been an attempt to reproduce the exact sound of the wind and the waves: a cymbal crash can never sound just like a splash; but it can suggest one. A work of art is not a slavish copy of nature; it is artificial in the original sense of the word, which means "made with skill." Whether he is a composer or a painter, an artist needs to have courage and imagination as well as energy and skill, for he has to create something that will not only have a life of its own, with the vitality of nature, but will also last for centuries.

A painted wave can give us such a vivid impression of the sea that we can almost feel the weight of the water and the sting of the spray. A real wave breaks and disperses; the painted wave remains poised, and yet exciting, for as long as there are people to look at it. The sound of a real wave breaking may never happen again in just that way, but the sounds a composer creates in a musical conversation between wind and waves can be repeated whenever there is an orchestra to play and an audience to listen.

The composer writes in the language of music, which can be as clear and concise as the language of words. Musicians who are thoroughly at home in their own language can read the printed symbols of sea music as easily as they can read printed words. There is no need for them to take the page to a piano and "try it over"; they can hear the sounds in their mind's ear. To those who cannot read the written language of music this may seem like magic. It is a matter of learning and practice—no more miraculous than being able to read Greek poetry, or to follow the symbols of algebra in an equation, or to understand the words in this sentence.

A painter paints on canvas with brushes and tubes of colored pigments, and with these simple, physical resources he creates art. In the same way, the resources of a composer are simple and physical; and all the sounds of a piece of music, high or low, loud or soft, long or short, quick or slow, can be written down on paper.

A sudden sound in the middle of a silence is like a pebble dropped into a pool; ripples travel outward from the center of disturbance. These ripples, or sound waves, reach the ear and, through it, the brain.

Strike a bell and touch it; its surface quivers with vibrations. It is even possible to see these vibrations, though their to-and-fro movements are so rapid that the bell may just look blurred. The distance to and fro that a vibrating surface moves from its position of rest is the *amplitude* of the vibration. The greater the amount of energy used to produce a vibration, the greater its amplitude will be; the greater the amplitude, the louder the sound will be.

Loudness can be scientifically measured in units called *decibels*, of which 1 represents the softest sound that the human ear can detect. A single decibel just crosses the threshold of hearing; any sound above 130 decibels, such as that of a low-flying plane, approaches the "threshold of pain."

To make a sound that we can hear, vibrations must be rapid. Our ears can hear sounds from about 20 to 20,000 vibrations per second. In *acoustics*☞, which is the science of hearing, the number of vibrations per second is called *frequency*; the greater the frequency, the higher the sound.

The height or depth of a sound is called *pitch*. Only regular vibrations of unvarying frequency produce a level of pitch. In speech the pitch is always varying. Say the word "no," trying to make it last more than five seconds without letting your voice go up or down. If the sound remains level you will no longer be speaking; you will be singing.

Above, Hokusai's Wave and Fujiyama; *the painter, like the composer, creates art with simple physical resources. Below, like ripples from a stone dropped in a pool, sound waves travel outward from a center of disturbance.*

When we listen to the birds singing we realize the innumerable possibilities of different levels of pitch. When human beings sing, they prefer to limit themselves to a small number of definite, easily recognizable levels of pitch. These are called *notes* or *tones*. Many of the familiar tunes that are whistled or sung throughout Europe and America are founded on only seven notes. These are the notes that can be heard in a chime of bells, running up and down the steps of a ladder of sounds; they can easily be picked out with one finger on the white keys of a piano.

You will find that the ladder of notes, 1, 2, 3, 4, 5, 6, 7, will sound incomplete without its eight step, called the *octave*. When the octave is added, you can play tunes, finding the notes by trial and error, while keeping the rhythm in mind.

Music, like dancing, moves through time. We can never hear the whole shape of a tune at once, or see the whole pattern of a dance in a single moment. But when a tune or a dance is over, we find that we still hold in our minds some of the pattern that we have been following.

Music sometimes flows freely, like conversation. More often its rhythm☞ is measured, like metrical verse, with a recurring pulse going through it. This pulse is not like the mechanical ticking of a clock, for rhythm is alive. It has physical tension and relaxation: a give-and-take as in the action of sawing a tree-trunk. When a swimmer learns to

Left, seven steps in the ladder of sound completed by the octave in a medieval chime of bells. Below, pipe and drum give the lively pulse for a dance.

swim he has to count to keep his movements rhythmical. Any continuous action, such as walking or running, becomes easier when it is done rhythmically. Rowers in a race keep time to the rhythm set by "stroke." Men hauling a rope avoid wasting energy by timing their efforts and pulling as one man. In parts of Africa where farm work is not yet mechanized, men often work in a rhythmical line, timing their steps so as to stamp the earth simultaneously. If they kept rigidly to a slow, monotonous "STAMP . . . STAMP . . . STAMP . . ." the distance to be covered might seem endless. So they vary the rhythm, making a time-pattern with steps that are half as slow as a stamp and with hops that are twice as quick as a step. Or they may choose to divide the pulse into threes, and to use their step and hop to create an entirely different time-pattern, as in skipping. There are endless possibilities when one begins inventing time-patterns like these. However elaborate the rhythms may be, the units of time that make up each pattern can always be counted in twos or threes, or in multiples of two or three.

People who have studied African customs have described how field workers will take a drummer with them to help them by beating out a rhythm that keeps them going for hour after hour. When they work in this way there is little difference between the rhythm of their work and the rhythm of a dance. The earliest dances we know anything about

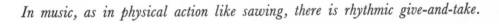

In music, as in physical action like sawing, there is rhythmic give-and-take.

Above, Cretan harvesters of c. 1500 B.C. in ritual procession. Below, ditchers working to the music of pipes in modern Haiti.

were rituals to bring back the spring after winter, to make the crops grow, and to celebrate the harvest. Ritual is still an important part of civilized life in the Far East, and even in Europe we can find scattered survivals of ancient spring dances.

In ritual dances rhythm is never casual: each step is important, for the dance may represent a matter of life and death. In our own music, rhythm is equally important: as soon as it becomes casual, the sound is not worth listening to. An orchestral drummer, unlike a ritual dancer, reads his time-patterns from a printed page, but unless he plays with the purposeful vitality of a ritual dancer the music will not come to life.

Time-patterns are written with symbols that correspond with dancers' stamp, step, hop. These symbols are referred to as "notes," as they represent notes of different lengths. The method of writing them is described as *notation*. Written notes of any length can be placed high or low, in various definite positions, to represent all the different levels of pitch that may be needed in tunes that are to be played or sung.

An orchestral drummer plays time-patterns read from the printed page.

2 Songs and Singers

The first European songs to be written down were Greek songs; and it is from the Greeks that we have learned to call notes of different pitch after the first seven letters of the alphabet—A, B, C, D, E, F, and G. Greek scholars, who studied music as a branch of mathematics, measured the distance from one note to another between each of the eight rungs in a ladder of sound. The step between rungs B and C and between E and F is only half the size of the other steps, and so it is called a *semitone*. A to B, C to D, D to E, and F to G are *whole tones*. We can see and hear the difference on the piano: it has no black key between B and C or E and F.

The ladder, or *scale*, of seven notes and the octave can begin on any note. The position of the semitones is one of the most important things in all music; for the tunes can grow out of scales, and the shape and character of a tune depends to a large extent on where its semitones occur. Many of the tunes we sing today are founded on the C to C scale, with the semitones between the third and fourth, and between the seventh and eighth steps or degrees. Other tunes, particularly some of the traditional folksongs that go back for hundreds of years, are founded on other natural scales or *modes*, such as from A to A, or from D to D.

The earliest European music that we know about was sung in Christian churches. It was a form of chanting, in which long sentences were sung on one note with occasional embellishments for the important words. Most of the texts for chanting were taken from the Book of Psalms, where the vivid language helped to transform spoken words into sung phrases. From the simple recitation of the psalms, chanting developed into extended lines of freely flowing melody. Singers no longer kept to one note for each syllable, but allowed their voices to rise and fall in an uninterrupted stream of sound on such singable words as "Alleluia" or "Amen." Hundreds of melodies were invented. In the 6th century, Pope Gregory collected all the existing chants and arranged them in the order in which they are still sung every Sunday in Roman Catholic churches and cathedrals throughout the world. By the end of the 6th century there were so many Gregorian chants that nobody could remember them all. These melodies, which we call *plainchant*, had to be written down. The Church's first experimental musical notation was a series of short curves that followed the rise and fall of the voices: the curves were called neumes from the Greek word for a sign. By the 10th century, a horizontal line was added, running from beginning to end of the chant, with a letter against it to show what level of pitch the line represented. This letter was called the *clef*, as it was the key to the position of the semitones. F and C were then the only letters used for clefs. In the 11th and 12th centuries, three more lines were added. These four parallel lines were called the *staff* or *stave*.

By this time musicians used square notes instead of neumes: they were written either on the lines or in the spaces. The clefs could be written on any line of the stave.

This sytem of notation is not unlike the one we use today. We have now added a fifth line to the stave, and our notes are oval in shape, instead of square. The F clef is always put on the fourth line from the bottom of the stave; it is called the *bass clef* because it is used for all lower voices and instruments. We still occasionally use the C clef, on the third or fourth line, for instruments of middle range, and we have added a third clef, the G clef, which is written on the second line of the stave; it is called the *treble clef* because it is used for all higher voices and instruments.

Musicians owe a debt of gratitude to the 11th-century scholar Guido of Arezzo, who invented movable names for the steps or degrees of the scale. He took the first syllable of each line of a well-known hymn to St. John that happened to have a tune moving up one note higher on every phrase:

"UT-queant laxis, RE-sonare fibris, MI-ra gestorum,
FA-muli tuorum, SOL-ve polluti, LA-bii reatum."

("That with easy voice Thy servants may be able to sing the wonders of Thy deeds, remove all sin from their polluted lips.") The note UT was the focal point of the tune; the other notes were sung in relation to it.

This is the system on which our modern tonic sol-fa is founded. It helped the monks of the Middle Ages to read unfamiliar chants on their journeys in foreign countries, and it lightened the task of those who

Above, ancient Greek sculpture of a poet-musician performing. Below, early Christians chanted the psalms in their high, resonant churches.

spent the whole of their lives copying illuminated manuscripts of Gregorian plainchant.

Until the middle of the 9th century, church music had consisted of a single line of melody, sung by one voice or by a choir. Then, in about 850, groups of singers began to experiment with two notes at the same time, finding that the combined sound, or *interval*, was more resonant.

Intervals are described as a second, a third, a fourth, and so on—counting up the scale from the lower note to the upper note. The size of some of the intervals varies according to where the semitones occur: larger intervals are called *major*, smaller are called *minor*.

Some intervals are called *dissonant*; they sound so uncomfortable that we want to move on somewhere else. *Consonant* intervals sound comfortable. Octaves, fifths, and fourths are perfect consonances; seconds and sevenths are dissonances. Somewhere between these are thirds and sixths: imperfect consonances. On a well-tuned piano we can hear the slight buzz of the thirds and sixths, and feel the discomfort of the seconds and sevenths.

It was in the 9th century that people began singing plainchant in *parallel motion* in intervals a fourth or a fifth apart. They also sang in *oblique motion*, with one voice holding the same note while the other voice went up or down, sometimes passing through all the intervals, according to the shape of the melodic line of the plainchant.

Medieval church musicians singing plainsong from manuscript notation.

In the 11th century, musicians made the important discovery of *contrary motion*, with one voice going up and the other voice coming down. This added a new dimension to the art of music; from then onward voices became more and more independent in their relations with each other. In the 12th century, the music of "note-against-note," or *counterpoint*, changed from the freely flowing rhythm of plainchant to a rhythm with a regular pulse divided into twos or threes. As counterpoint developed, a third voice was added, and then a fourth. In the 13th century, musicians found that several voices could begin one after another on the same tune, imitating each other as we do today when we sing *rounds*. This was one of the most exciting discoveries in European music.

In all these experiments the medieval Church was the unrivaled patron of music, as of all the other arts. People also sang secular music. Very little is known of the minstrels who went from one castle to another singing ballads, for the tunes were not written down. The first secular songs to be written down were those of the troubadours and trouvères, who were aristocratic poet-musicians living in France in the 12th and 13th centuries. Their songs were nearly always about the joys of spring or the unsurpassable beauty of their exquisite ladies. The fashion for these songs spread to other countries. The German troubadours were called minnesingers, "Minne" meaning "courtly love."

Left, an early-15th-century round, with one voice coming in after another. Right, 13th-century Spanish musicians playing early stringed instruments.

stella. dei mater alma. atq3

semp virgo felix celi porta.

Left, a plainsong hymn to the Virgin, from an illuminated manuscript of 1415. Above, secular music-making in a castle garden in medieval France.

The troubadours and minnesingers kept to a single line of melody in their songs; but secular rounds were already being sung in the 14th century, the most famous being the English round "Sumer is icumen in."

The secular counterpoint of the Middle Ages helped to bring into being the new music of the Renaissance, which reached its Golden Age in the middle of the 16th century, when there were so many great composers that it would take any present-day musician a long lifetime to get to know all their works.

The printing of music had been invented in the 15th century; and by the time of the Golden Age it was possible for ordinary people to sing counterpoint in their own homes. They used to sit around the table after a meal, often sharing one music book between them, its pages printed so that each singer had the notes of his own part facing him. The contrapuntal songs they sang were called *madrigals*, which means that they were in the mother tongue. The notes and rhythms of their interweaving lines of melody were often intricate, and there must have been frequent occasions when the singers lost their places and had to begin again.

It was considered a social disgrace not to be able to read music at sight, just as it was a disgrace not to know the steps and the figures of the fashionable dances of the time. Such dances were the Pavane, "staid and grave"; the Galliard, which could be either lively or graceful; the Coranto, "full of sprightliness and vigour"; and the Lavolta, a favorite with Queen Elizabeth I, in which the ladies were thrown up into the air and bounced about until they were dizzy in the head.

Many of the later madrigals were founded on dance-rhythms. In these short part-songs the voices abandoned their independence and drew together on the main pulse of the music, keeping to a simple rhythm for the refrain of "Fa la la" at the end of each verse. This dancing rhythm was one cause of an epoch-making change in music that happened in the late 16th century. Instead of listening mostly to the long, horizontal, interwoven threads of counterpoint, musicians began to listen more to the combined vertical intervals they were singing. These combined intervals are called *chords*☞. Moving from one chord to another is *harmony*☞. As soon as composers began writing music in harmony rather than in counterpoint, they discarded the modal scales of the early church music and wrote either in the *C* to *C* mode, called the *major* scale, or in a version of the *A* to *A* mode, called the *minor* scale.

The change-over from counterpoint to harmony had far-reaching effects on the whole of European music. One of the immediate results was that people making music in their homes preferred to sing to the accompaniment of instruments.

AVDITVS.
L'OVYE.

Left, an informal group of amateur singers and players in a 16th-century home. Above, the dances of the Renaissance were sprightly, vigorous, and gay. Below, a 16th-century madrigal printed to be sung around a table.

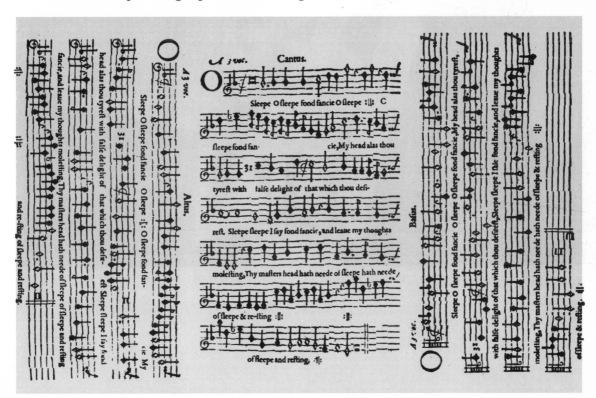

3   Instruments and Players

Anything that sets up sound vibrations can become an instrument. A hollow tree can be hit with a stick; a hollow bamboo can be blown into; the trip-thong of a hunter's snare can be plucked. We can experiment with these jungle methods by tapping the surface of a table with a pencil, or blowing suddenly into the cap of a fountain-pen, or stretching a thin rubber band as far as it will go and twitching it with a finger or thumb.

Modern orchestral instruments are divided into three main categories: those that are hit are *percussion* instruments; those that are blown are *wind* instruments; and those that can be plucked or scraped are *string* instruments. Within each main division there are family groups, each member having its own characteristic voice that is easy to recognize.

The characteristic sound of an instrument depends upon its shape and size, the materials out of which it is made, the particular device that sets it vibrating, and the audibility of its faint overtones called *harmonics*.

The chief percussion instrument is the *drum*. Its vibrating surface is a skin that is tightly stretched across the open ends of a hollow, resonant cylinder. Modern drums are played with soft-headed sticks. *Side-drums* have pencil-thin sticks that make a brittle sound. Other orchestral percussion instruments are the *triangle*, which clinks; the *tambourine*, which jingles; and the *castanets*, which clack. *Cymbals*, large plates of brass, can be clashed together. When a player holds up one cymbal and touches it with a soft-headed stick, it makes a bell-like sound.

Chiming *bells* in an orchestra are now tubular instead of bell-shaped: their harmonics are so audible that they often sound like complicated chords. The *gong* is loud enough to drown all other orchestral notes. It must never be played too violently, for the sound is powerful enough to cross the threshold of pain, and could deafen a listener for life.

The only members of the orchestra that can compare in power with the percussion are the *brass* wind instruments. All the brass instruments consist of a long tube with a cupped mouthpiece. A player can get any harmonic by altering the pressure of his lips: the greater the pressure, the higher the harmonic. The familiar notes of a *trumpet* fanfare owe their brilliance to the clear, energetically produced harmonics. No other instrument can sound so triumphant.

Horns can also sound brilliant, though some of their most characteristic notes are in the mellow range of the lower harmonics. In modern orchestras the horns and trumpets are no longer limited to the "open" notes of the harmonic series; they are able to get all the remaining notes with the help of three pistons, or *valves*, which let in extra bits of tube to lower the pitch when required. *Trombones* do not need valves, as they have a separate length of tubing that slides in and out, enabling them to get all the notes they need. Trombones can be played as brilliantly as trumpets, but they can also sound solemn.

Woodwind instruments are more gentle in sound than the brass. Gentlest of all is the flute. The primitive ancestor of the flute family was

a one-note pipe made of bone or bamboo. The pitch of its note depended on the length of the pipe. When several pipes of different lengths were joined side by side, as in the instrument called the panpipes, it became possible to play tunes. A better way of getting different notes was discovered by taking a single pipe and boring holes at various distances along it. Each hole altered the length of the vibrating column of air in the instrument, so that the notes of a scale could be played by covering all the holes with the fingers and then lifting one finger after another. This is the method that is still used, though modern flutes have metal levers called keys that cover the holes. The connecting mechanism of these keys makes it easier to play music that needs intricate fingering. The flute is held crosswise: the player does not cover the mouth-hole, but lets his breath strike the edge of it. The end-blown flute, called the *recorder,* is a relation of the orchestral transverse flute. The recorder is the easiest of the woodwind instruments for beginners to learn to play.

A grass-blade or a reed, held between two thumbs and blown upon, will produce a shrill squawk. A reed stuck into the end of a bamboo pipe makes a primitive reed instrument. It is the ancestor of our modern *oboe,* which can sound more expressive than any other woodwind instrument. Instruments of the modern oboe family, which includes the *cor anglais* and *bassoon,* have double reeds that vibrate against each other. The *clarinet,* which has evolved from the "drone" of the bagpipes, has a single reed. The clarinet's lowest notes are dark, the middle notes are mellow, while the highest notes can sound like distant trumpets.

Far left, drums beat the rhythm for a dance. Left, a set of bells. Below, 16th-century trumpeters and drummers of the Holy Roman Emperor.

Of all the stringed instruments, the *harp* is probably the oldest that is still played. Each string of a harp has its own note: the longer the string, the lower the pitch. The Greeks played the harp and also the lyre, with strings of the same length, but strung at different tensions.

Plucked instruments of many shapes are still played in all Eastern countries. The Arabian "al'ud" is the direct ancestor of the European *lute*—an instrument with a hollow pear-shaped body that was to be found in every musician's home during the 16th century. Unfortunately there are very few 20th-century lute players, but the *guitar*, a member of the same family, is a very popular instrument.

The first bowed instrument also came from Arabia. It was called the rebab, and it reached medieval Europe as the rebeck. European craftsmen soon improved the tone of their bowed instruments. They made them in different sizes, so that by the 16th century it was possible to play contrapuntal string music in several parts. The new instruments were called *viols*—the treble, alto, tenor, and bass viol corresponding, though not very closely, to our *violin*, *viola*, *cello*, and *bass*.

Opposite: above left, a Japanese transverse flute; right, a modern oboe; beneath, an ancient Egyptian harp player. Below, Renaissance chamber music.

Greek engineers invented the first *organ*, an instrument with the name "hydraulis," which resembled a large set of panpipes with a wind-supply worked by water-pressure. From A.D. 400 onward the wind for this earliest of all keyboard instruments was provided by bellows. Our modern organs are electrically blown, with pedals for the feet and several keyboards, or *manuals*, for the hands. Hundreds of pipes enable the player to reach from the lowest bass to the highest treble, and to vary the sound from the whisper of a flute to the flourish of trumpets.

The earliest stringed keyboard instrument is the *clavichord*, which dates from the 14th century. It is ideal for playing at home, as its expressive notes are so quiet that they cannot be heard in the next room. The *harpsichord*, dating from the 16th century, can vary its tone from a delicate lute-like whisper to a brilliant sparkling sonority, but on even the most highly developed 18th-century harpsichord it was not possible to change from loud to soft within one short phrase. This is a characteristic of the modern *piano*, which was called the *pianoforte* because it can play both softly and loudly without extra machinery.

Music-making in the home has flourished ever since the 16th century. Amateurs who lived during the Renaissance were particularly fortunate, as they had so many great composers writing instrumental music for them to play. Sixteenth-century chamber-music was mostly played by groups of viols or recorders. Brass instruments were unsuitable for chamber music as they were too loud to be played in a small room: they belonged to open-air processions in the streets or to festive occasions in cathedrals or in spacious banqueting halls.

Toward the end of the 16th century, composers began combining different groups of instruments in the same piece of music. In their extended choral works they placed brass, woodwind, and strings in the different galleries of a cathedral, alternating the groups for contrasts of loud and soft music. On other occasions a composer would gather all his instrumentalists around him and would direct them from the harpsichord, transforming them into an *orchestra*.

Left, a Flemish spinet of about 1600, *made of wood inlaid with ivory. Above,* The Concert *by the* 17th-*century Dutch painter Gerard Terborch.*

4   Drama in Music

The golden age of Renaissance music coincided with a golden age of drama: but it was not until the end of the 16th century that anyone thought of bringing the two arts together. Music in a Shakespeare play is incidental. There are fanfares of trumpets for the approach of a king, drum-rolls for a funeral, dances for a wedding, and songs sung to the lute during a love scene: but no one would have thought of trying to sing the words of the dramatic dialogues or the poetic soliloquies.

At the end of the 16th century several Italian poets, artists, actors, and musicians met together in a Florentine palace to discuss the possibility of creating a musical style similar to what they imagined the choruses in Greek tragedy might have sounded like. This was the beginning of *opera*. The scripts, or *librettos*, were especially written to be set to music. Actors abandoned the wide apron stages of the 16th-century theatre and concentrated their gestures within the framework of a proscenium arch. Costumes and settings were pastoral or heroic in character, and the music was a sung declamation, called *recitative*, which followed the natural rhythm of the spoken words.

Recitative was accompanied by a harpsichord and a bass viol. The composer wrote the bass notes of the accompaniment and added numerical figures in a kind of musical shorthand to show what chords were to be played. The notes of a chord could be spaced in any order above the bass, and there was no need to play them simultaneously: they could be spread out slowly or broken up into harp-like cascades called *arpeggios* to add to the dramatic effect of the words in the recitative.

In this kind of accompaniment, called *figured bass*, the keyboard player was free to improvise his own part as he went along, provided that he kept to the right chords. While realizing the composer's intentions he could also follow the singer's gestures, and give him sympathetic and flexible support in all the changing moods of his song.

The first outstandingly great composer of opera was Claudio Monteverdi, who lived and worked in Venice in the early 17th century. He used exciting instrumental accompaniment in his operatic songs, which were called *arias*, and he developed the harmonies of his figured basses so that he could convey any mood of the drama with a few chords.

Opera was brought into France by a young Florentine composer called Lully, who became a naturalized Frenchman and a court musician to Louis XIV. Ballets were then the fashion in Paris; and by introducing a large number of dances into his pastoral operas, Lully became a popular success as a composer. He was himself an actor and a dancer. He invented the minuet, which was said to be the French king's favorite dance.

Opera reached England in the second half of the 17th century, when the stage entertainments called masques were becoming transformed into dramatic works with continuous music. The great English opera composer was Henry Purcell. He had an astonishingly keen sense of the musical possibilities of his native language. His settings of descriptive adjectives, such as "triumphant" or "drooping," are so vivid that they almost convey actual gestures. He gave the characters in his dramas a musical personality that was subtler and more distinctive than anything the spoken libretto could give them. He died at the age of 36, having written incidental music for 50 plays, as well as the opera *Dido and Aeneas*, which is his masterpiece.

In Italy the operatic tradition begun by Monteverdi was continued in the late 17th and 18th centuries by the Neapolitan composer Alessandro Scarlatti and his son Domenico. Alessandro has been described as the originator of *bel canto*, a singing technique that emphasized beauty of tone and brilliance of performance, and which has remained an ideal for many opera singers. Italy was considered to be the center of musical life during the 18th century. Throughout Europe, the very words describing the way in which a piece of music should be performed were written in Italian: we still use such words as *vivace* (lively) and *accelerando* (getting quicker).

The most famous 18th-century composer of Italian opera was Handel, who was born in Germany and later naturalized as an Englishman. He spent a great deal of his life traveling and must have felt at home in any country in Europe. He had met Domenico Scarlatti in Rome when they were both in their early twenties, and had been fired with enthusiasm for the *bel canto* of the Neapolitan school.

Above, a contemporary portrait of Monteverdi, the first great opera composer. Below, the opening of a lively song by the English opera composer Purcell.

SOLO.   A *single* SONG.

/Ark! hark! the ecch'ing Air a tri - - - - - - umph sings,   hark! the

Above, the performance of an opera by Lully, himself an actor and dancer and the inventor of the Minuet. Below, an early 18th-century opera rehearsal.

Handel wrote more than 40 operas. Not many of them are performed today, partly because of the technical difficulties of some of the vocal writing. Many of his operas called for highly elaborate scenery and stage effects; in his stage directions we find statues rising from a trapdoor surrounded by fire, while cupids fly about in mid-air. Many 18th-century operatic conventions now seem pointless. One that was rigidly observed throughout Handel's life was that after a solo aria the singer must immediately go off into the wings. This meant that when the hero had proposed to the heroine he had to walk off and leave her without waiting for her answer. Composer and librettist had to put up with this absurd situation, because the performers insisted on having an opportunity for prolonged applause at the end of every song. Opera singers were the popular stars of their time—and they could be very temperamental, especially during rehearsals.

Although Handel's operas are largely forgotten, his *oratorios* are still frequently performed, particularly his *Messiah*. An oratorio is like a religious opera but without action or scenery or costumes: all the drama is concentrated in the music. In Handel's oratorios there are amazingly dramatic moments, such as the scene in *Samson* where the recitative is suddenly interrupted by frantic scale passages in the orchestra, which give a vivid impression of the collapse of the Temple and the destruction of the crowd of Philistines.

Although Handel traveled so much, he never met his famous German contemporary, Bach, who was the greatest of all writers of dramatic religious music. Bach was born into a large family of hard-working

Elaborate costumes and a stage "giant" in Handel's opera Ptolomeo.

Left, the performance of a cantata in a German church at the time of Bach. Above, part of the manuscript of Handel's Messiah, *written in his own hand.*

musicians: he must have heard music all day long while still in his cradle. As a young man he studied the instrumental music of the Italian composer Vivaldi, rewriting his string orchestral works so that they could be played on the harpsichord. He also learned a great deal from the music of the Scandinavian composer Buxtehude: on one occasion he walked 200 miles in order to listen to Buxtehude playing the organ.

Bach lived in Germany all his life, earning his living as a provincial organist and choirmaster. The works, called *cantatas*, that he wrote for his Sunday services were like oratorios on a small scale. They usually began with a chorus, with orchestral accompaniment, founded on a familiar Lutheran hymn-tune. This would be followed by solo arias linked by short recitatives, ending with a straightforward version of the hymn-tune in which the congregation could sing with the choir.

The congregation could also join in the hymns in Bach's settings of the Passion. The tenor soloist sang the words of the Evangelist in dramatic recitative, describing each incident in the story, and leading up to the direct quotations of the words of Christ or Pilate, which were sung by other solo voices. The chorus represented the crowds in the angry scenes outside the judgment-hall and at the Crucifixion. The counterpoint in these crowd scenes, as in much of Bach's music, was in a style called *fugal*, which means that the voices followed each other in close imitation, just as an idea passes from person to person in a crowd.

5 Styles in Music

When Bach died in 1750 his music was already considered to be out of fashion. His own sons were no longer satisfied with composing fugues☞: their father had been writing fugues superbly for nearly half a century and they felt the time had come for a change. They revered his music and his memory, but they knew that as young composers they must explore the new music that was being written and find their own way about in it. So they broke away from harmonic counterpoint and began writing in a new style.

There is no such thing as a straight path of progress in music, beginning in some remote, primitive past and stretching onward and upward to some far-distant perfection. Instead, the history of music moves up and down and to and fro, with unexpected changes of style, as in any other art. These changes may be seen particularly clearly in architecture, where styles can alternate between highly decorated and severely plain. New fashions in clothes may coincide with a complete change of style in dancing; which means that there will also be a change of style in music, since dancing and music are inseparably linked together.

The far-reaching change that took place in the style of music about 1750 was largely the result of a change in musical patronage. For hundreds of years the Church had been the chief patron of musicians. But Bach was the last of the great composers who managed to earn his living in full-time employment by church authorities. The new patrons were the rich princes and landowners who liked to have a resident composer working for them so that they and their guests could enjoy listening to music every evening. They employed their own orchestras of skilled instrumentalists, and built their own small opera-houses, for private performances of chamber operas. These connoisseurs wanted courteous formality in music; so their composers evolved new styles for them— "galant," elegant, and unruffled.

The first of the great composers to write music in the late 18th-century style was Haydn. As a young student in Vienna he had studied the works of one of Bach's sons, and had taught himself to write in the new classical *sonata form*. This meant using contrasting tunes, breaking them up into fragments, working up to a climax of suspense; and then returning to the original opening in its straightforward simplicity, with a tail-piece, or *coda*, to show that the musical journey was at an end.

Haydn was employed on the country estate of the Esterhazy family, where he spent 30 years in the Prince's household, writing and rehearsing and performing music for the enjoyment of the guests, and providing whatever kind of entertainment was required; he even wrote the tunes for the musical clocks that chimed the hours in the state apartments. In his chamber music he made use of whatever instrumentalists were available, and soon discovered that the combined sound of two violins, a viola, and a cello was just right for the new form, with its many possibilities for intimate musical conversations. This was the birth of the *string quartet*.

Mozart, the greatest of all the 18th-century classical composers, said that it was from Haydn that he first learned the true way to compose quartets. Mozart had been an infant prodigy. He was famous throughout Europe, not only as a composer but also as a performer on the newly invented pianoforte. But in spite of this he was never able to earn an adequate living, for he insisted on working independently, without regular patrons. His father, who was a violin teacher, tried to persuade him to take pupils, but the 22-year-old Mozart refused, saying: "I am a composer and I neither can nor ought to bury the talent with which God in His goodness has so richly endowed me. I may say so without conceit, for I feel it now more than ever."

His success with audiences was often great, and tunes from his operas were whistled through the streets of half a dozen capital cities of Europe. Best of all, his fellow musicians recognized his genius. An eye-witness account of the first performance of his opera *Figaro* describes how the members of the orchestra went on and on applauding the composer, "beating the bows of their violins against the music desks."

With the fame of Haydn and Mozart, Vienna became the capital of the musical world and attracted a young German composer from Bonn. This was Beethoven, whose genius allowed his dynamic emotions to break the hitherto unruffled surface of late 18th-century music.

The 18th century had already come to an end by the time another Viennese, Schubert, began composing. Like Mozart, Schubert chose to

Mozart, at the age of seven, making music with his father and sister.

Above, the opening of a Mozart quartet, in his own handwriting. Below, the first performance in 1775 of a Haydn opera in the Esterhazy Theatre.

work without any regular patron, and refused to spend his time teaching in a school. Schubert's music was seldom performed in public during his short lifetime; but poets, painters, and musicians used to crowd into a small room, week after week, to hear him accompany his friend Vogl in the songs he had just been writing, for they knew that "everything he touched turned to music."

Nineteenth-century music is often called "romantic"—a difficult word to define. To the German poets and musicians of the early 19th century it meant escape from the ordinary everyday world, into what they imagined the Romanesque world of the 12th century might have been like, with its troubadours and minstrels, its knights in armor and ladies in tall, pointed hats, and its dark forests and high-towered castles. The first flowering of pure romantic music was the opera *Der Freischütz* by the German composer Carl Maria von Weber, which has a scene of magic and horror in the Wolf's Glen.

Throughout most of the century, piano pieces were written with descriptive titles such as *Early Morning in Spring*, *The Haymakers*, or *Forest Murmurs*. These pieces were practiced by solitary piano pupils—a complete contrast to music-making in the home in earlier centuries, when everyone had taken it for granted that amateur music was an occupation to be shared with other people.

A drawing by one of Schubert's friends, showing the scene at a "Schubert evening" in Vienna, with poets, painters, and musicians listening to Schubert playing the music he had just been composing.

Professional combined music-making was on a very much larger scale than ever before: huge choirs and orchestras of over a thousand performers gathered together in vast concert halls. Solo instrumentalists were now the famous stars. The works they played with orchestral accompaniment, called *concertos*, had little in common with the chamber concertos of Mozart or of Bach, where a soloist used to sit in the middle of a small group of instrumentalists, often sharing a music-stand with the player sitting next to him.

Nineteenth-century virtuoso performers, such as the violinist Paganini or the pianist-composer Liszt, were placed well in front of the ordinary members of the orchestra; and the works they played gave them frequent opportunities for displaying their unrivaled technical powers. Rapturous crowds followed them wherever they went, carrying them triumphantly through the streets of European capitals or strewing thousands of rose-petals at their feet.

The form of the music they played was still recognizable as having been adapted from the 18th-century classical sonata form of the Viennese school. But the mood of courteous formality was now transformed into a warmth that expressed the composer's personal emotions.

Opera singers now had to contend with a much more powerful orchestra. They needed to be physically tough to endure the strain of having to sing, for three hours, against the sustained resonance and the passionate outbursts of their orchestral accompaniment.

An orchestral rehearsal in Switzerland in the late 1930s.

A page from a modern score for full orchestra.

6   East and West

Listening for the first time to an Indian musician singing or playing, a musician of the West is more than likely to feel bewildered, for the sound is utterly different from anything he has heard before. The tone seems harsh and the notes slide up and down in a manner that would never be tolerated in Europe or America. But the Indian musician may be just as bewildered by Western music. He will certainly be shocked by the out-of-tune division of the octave into 12 *equal-tempered* semitones.

The seven notes of the Indian scale are called by the Sanskrit syllables SA RE GA MA PA DHA NI (corresponding to our UT RE MI FA SOL LA SI), but of these notes only SA and PA remain at the same pitch, whatever the tune may be. The other scale degrees are flattened or sharpened according to what mode the music is in.

The single melodic line of Indian music is never harmonized with chords: it is accompanied by elaborate drum-rhythms that Europeans find exciting to listen to but difficult to follow. It is only after getting rid of all set notions of what music ought to sound like, that the Western listener can accept Indian music with an open ear.

One of the most obvious differences between Eastern and Western music is the way in which it is presented. In a Western orchestra, performers are placed on a platform in front of straight rows of listeners; they spend several minutes tuning their instruments; they open their printed copies of music at the right page; the conductor walks on to the platform to a loud burst of applause; he raises his baton; and the concert begins.

In India, the performers sit cross-legged on the floor in the small space left by the semicircle of listeners. The drummer may take half an hour to get his instrument in tune; no one is impatient, for this is part of the ceremony of music-making. There are no written notes, for the music gradually emerges as an improvisation. There is no clapping, for it is considered barbarous; but at an exciting climax or a subtly turned phrase in the music the members of the audience show their obvious delight.

Eastern music has its roots in ceremony. Chinese music has traditions that can be traced back for at least 4000 years, when the sacred gong, called "huang chung," gave the correct pitch to which all other instruments were tuned. Instruments were divided into eight traditional categories according to the materials they were made of; and each instrument was related to a point of the compass, a season of the year, and an aspect of nature such as fire, water, or thunder.

In the T'ang Dynasty (A.D. 618-907) ceremonial music was performed by orchestras of 300 players. The tunes they played were founded on a five-note gapped scale without any semitones. You can try it out on the black keys of the piano, and you will be surprised at the number of different tunes these five notes can make, especially if you vary the shape of the scale by beginning on a different note.

Very little of the ceremonial music of China has survived, but some Chinese traditions have been preserved in the court and temple music of Japan. This music is played on a small orchestra of flutes, oboes, lutes, drums, gongs, and a kind of mouth organ that has a cluster of reed pipes sticking out of a gourd-shaped bowl. Traditional Japanese music also includes the dramatic chanting of the *No* plays—a ceremonial form of theatrical entertainment that has existed for at least a thousand years and is still performed today.

The most exciting traditional orchestras in the Far East are the "gamelan" orchestras of Java and Bali. They consist of a number of percussion instruments made of different materials such as bamboo, wood, stone, and bronze. The largest instruments play the slowest notes; the smallest play quick patterns around the five notes of the scale on which the whole of the music is founded.

This elaborately organized variety that grows out of a few simple notes is the main characteristic of Eastern music. When an Indian singer and his drummer begin to improvise they are not plunging into the unknown and trusting to luck that they will keep together. They are starting with a given "raga," which is a fixed melodic formula appropriate to a particular time of the day and season of the year, and they develop it according to tradition, sometimes taking two or three hours over it, offering suggestions to each other and working up to tremendous climaxes with the freedom born of confidence.

Above, a Balinese gamelan *orchestra. Below, a snake-charming class in India.*

Above, a scene from a Japanese Nō play. Below, a Chinese orchestra.

"Janosik with his band," a Slovakian folk painting of musicians performing.

It was in the 19th century that Western composers first took any real interest in Eastern music. They were beginning to think about national characteristics in music and were exploring the folksongs of their own countries and introducing them into their works. Russian composers, who used folk music from Central Asia and Asia Minor, were among the first to write in a deliberately national style. When Central European countries followed their example, they found that their own folksongs had often got mixed up with the music of the gypsies, and they could not always tell which was which.

No one knows for certain where the gypsies came from. They were an Indian race, traveling from east to west, bringing with them their own language but borrowing almost everything else from the country they were passing through. The gypsies used an Indian scale, C D flat E F G A flat B C, for rhythmic incantations in their fortune-telling, and when they borrowed Romanian, Hungarian, and Slavonic folk-tunes for their songs and dances they adapted them to their own style, using flamboyant flourishes that belonged more to the East than to the West. This particular style suited the violin better than any other instrument. Gypsy violinists became internationally famous: Haydn heard them when they were invited to Esterhazy, and Schubert listened to them while sitting with his friends in the cafés of Vienna. Later in the 19th century, several composers, including Liszt and Brahms, wrote Rhapsodies founded on gypsies' versions of Central European tunes.

In Spain the gypsies found folk-tunes that were already Eastern in origin. The Moors had brought their own musical instruments into

Spain, and their traditions never died out: the songs we now describe as "flamenco" are still sung with their opening words in Arabic.

Flamenco has become popular in the United States of America, where the national music has grown from traditional European tunes and, in particular, from the folk music of Africa. When the Civil War was over, groups of Negroes traveling from one small town to another attracted crowds of listeners when they sang their "spiritual" songs, adapting the harmonies they had heard during missionary services. There was a deep melancholy in their singing, which colored their descriptions of crossing the river Jordan and of the long journey through the wilderness to the Promised Land.

The Negroes also sang work-songs while picking cotton in the fields or working on the railroads: these were later transformed into American "shouts," "walk-arounds," and "field-hollers."

In all their songs and dances, the negroes never lost the wonderful sense of rhythm they had inherited from their ancestors in Africa. The time-patterns owed much of their excitement to *syncopation*, a rhythmical device for avoiding obviousness by finding unexpected accents between the main beats of the bar. This was the foundation of jazz.

Jazz has become a commercial industry: the excitement of improvisation is too often lost in the process of "canning"; and in much recorded jazz the rhythm has become routine. But when jazz is performed by an artist in his own surroundings the true rhythmic vitality remains.

Jazz has influenced many composers and has helped, in its own way, to bring about the new music of the 20th century.

Below, a street band playing in New Orleans. Right, singer Josh White.

7 Composer; Performer; Listener

When a composer sets out to write a piece of music he is usually quite definite about what he is going to create; for although music is intangible there is nothing vague about it. A composer has to be a practical workman. He may, for instance, be asked to write an opera for a particular occasion. For this he would need the help of many other practical artists. Here is the kind of way in which an opera could be made, from its very first idea to its actual presentation on the stage.

The composer will probably begin by drawing up a time schedule of work, as if he were an architect-builder. Then he finds the right librettist to work with, and they discuss the chosen story in detail, plan its general outline, and divide it into scenes—even into arias, recitatives, and choruses. When the librettist has written his first draft of the words the composer studies it, pointing out weak syllables that destroy the rhythm, or clusters of consonants that would be unsingable. As soon as the libretto is satisfactory the composer begins to set it to music, working at it day after day until it is finished.

He writes his first sketches in "short score," roughly indicating the instruments that are to play, but keeping the notes to two or three staves. When he gets to the end of each of the acts he plays it through on the piano to the producer and the principal singers in the cast.

The music is copied out and duplicated and the singers learn their parts. Meanwhile the scenery and costumes will have been designed: the designer will have had to work in close consultation with the producer, to avoid making mistakes—such as putting a solid piece of scenery where it prevents the heroine watching the conductor's beat.

The composer will by then have written the full score—a task that may take weeks or months of continual work, all day, every day, and half the night. He will then go through the score with the conductor; the parts will be copied; the orchestra will rehearse in the pit of the empty opera-house; and when the moment comes for the curtain to go up on the opening night, the combined efforts of all those taking part will bring the composer's ideas to life.

A painter hangs his finished picture on a wall, and everyone can see it. A composer writes a work, but no one can hear it until it is performed. Professional singers and players have great responsibilities; for the composer is utterly dependent on them. A student of music needs as long and as arduous a training to become a performer as a medical student needs to become a doctor. Most training is concerned with technique, for musicians have to have the muscular proficiency of an athlete or a ballet dancer. Singers practice breathing every day, as their vocal chords would be inadequate without controlled muscular support. String players practice moving the fingers of the left hand up and down, while drawing the bow to and fro with the right arm—two entirely different movements.

Singers and instrumentalists have to be able to get every note perfectly in tune. Pianists are spared this particular anxiety, for the notes are already there, waiting for them, and it is the piano-tuner's responsibility to tune their instrument for them. But they have their own difficulties: the hammers that hit the strings have to be coaxed not to sound like percussion, and each overlapping tune has to sound clear.

This problem of getting clear texture is one that confronts the student conductor: he has to learn to know every note of the music and how it should sound, and he has to aim at controlling these sounds with fanatical but selfless authority.

Technique is no use unless it is combined with musical knowledge and understanding. Great artists are those who are so thoroughly at home in the language of music that they can enjoy performing works written in any century.

During the last 60 or 70 years there has been a good deal of interest in the revival of early music. This has had one drawback: it has set up a false distinction between "music" and "contemporary music." Over a century ago there was no such barrier and "music" meant the music that was being written at the time. But in our own century most concert-goers think of contemporary music as something unusual—outside the normal repertoire. They prefer programs that keep to familiar composers such as Beethoven and Tchaikovsky.

Twentieth-century music has therefore started at a disadvantage. And, unfortunately, it has made matters worse for itself by often sounding so strange. Experiments have been made in three keys, in no keys, in

Above, the great Russian cellist Mstislav Rostropovitch playing music especially written for him. Below, part of a composer's first sketch for an opera.

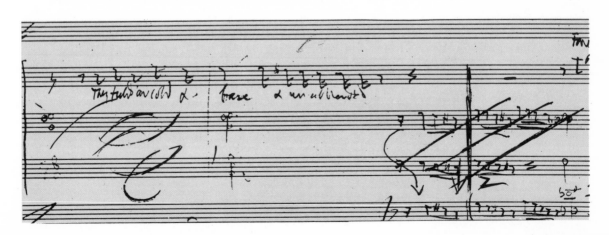

The stage design for Diaghilev's first production of Rimski-Korsakov's ballet
Le Coq d'Or *in Paris in 1914.*

quarter tones, in borrowing from ragtime and borrowing from blues, in Back-to-Bach, in machine music made out of gunfire, factory sirens, and ships' whistles. Some early 20th-century experiments have been short-lived; others, such as writing in two keys, have been absorbed into the music of today, where they no longer cause any discomfort to listeners.

One entirely new method of writing music has developed during the last half-century. This is the twelve-note method☞, which has broken right away from the traditions of 2000 years. The system is not founded on the seven-note scale with UT as its focal point; it is founded on the division of the octave into 12 notes a semitone apart, each note being equally important. The notes are arranged in a fixed order that can be used forward, backward, and upside-down as the material out of which "serial" music is constructed.

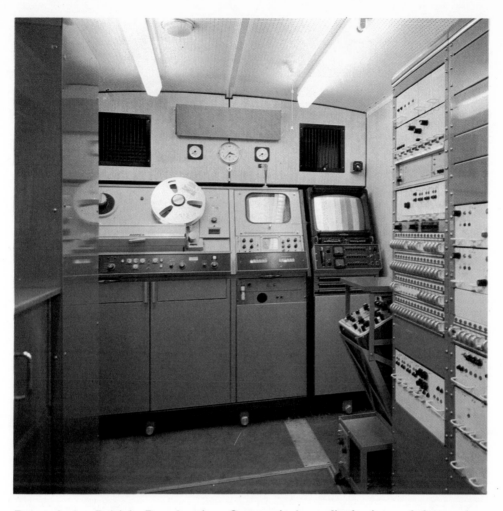

Part of the British Broadcasting Corporation's radiophonic workshop, where experiments are made with sounds produced electronically.

It is impossible for anyone to say whether this is to be the recognized music of the late 20th century. Some musicians think it is. Some think that there are still unlimited possibilities in the seven-note scale and the chords that grow out of it. Some think that it does not matter what style a composer chooses to write in, as long as he has something definite to say and says it clearly.

Future music historians, when they write about music in the 20th century, will have to describe many changes in the working lives of professional musicians and the ways in which they earned a living. Today, the great private patrons no longer exist. Rich enthusiasts can help by forming trusts to provide money for various forms of music-making, and large commercial firms sometimes organize concerts, or offer music scholarships, as part of their welfare services. The state itself has become a powerful patron, more powerful in some countries than in others. Many people worry about this question of state support for the arts—whether it should or should not be given and where the money is to come from. Without some such support, opera companies and orchestras would find it impossible to survive.

Since the middle of this century, the most usual way for professional musicians to earn their living has been by broadcasting and recording their performances. This means that they spend a good deal of time in sound-proof studios, singing or playing into a microphone, and they miss the necessary give-and-take between performer and listener.

The mechanical reproduction of sound has led to experiments in *electronic* music, and there are now many composers who are fascinated by the possibilities of sorting out extraordinary sounds that have never been heard before. The sounds are produced by electronic impulses, so there is no need for any human player.

The story of music does not come to an end with these electronic devices, for mechanized sound reproduction has had several other results, including a tremendous increase in the number of listeners who can enjoy hearing great music of any century. And there are members of these vast new audiences who are not content with sitting still and listening: they want to learn to sing and play. Music-making flourishes in many homes, in spite of what people say about this being an age of passive entertainment. The language of music is becoming more and more widely known. School orchestras are now taken just as much for granted as school classes in drawing and painting. Composers are writing for combined amateur choirs and orchestras, with choruses in which the audience is invited to join in the singing.

There can be no doubt that the present day is an exciting time for musicians, and there is a chance that we may soon find ourselves living in another golden age of music.

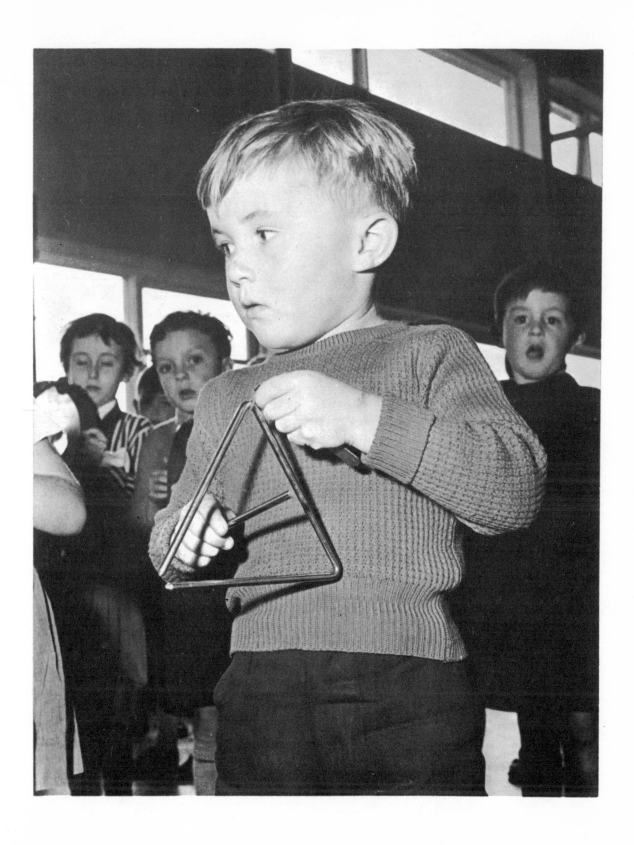

Glossary

In this Glossary, as in the rest of the book, the symbol ☞ means that the term it follows has its own alphabetical entry in the Glossary, to which you may refer for a fuller definition or for more information.

A   The first of the seven alphabetical letter-names, from A up to G, that are used to describe seven definite levels of sound in music. Each level of sound is a *note*, or a *tone*. The seven notes, A, B, C, D, E, F, G, can be found on the "white" notes of the piano.

The next "white" note above G is another A, an *octave* above the previous A. The lowest A and the highest A on the piano are seven octaves apart. The different octaves can be described as being above or below the C in the middle of the piano, which is called Middle C. The A above Middle C is the note that orchestral players listen to on a tuning fork when they are getting in tune to the right *pitch*, which is the word used for the height or depth of a sound.

ACOUSTICS   The science of sound. We hear a note being played or sung because sound waves reach our ears. The sound waves are caused by the vibrations of a stretched string when it is plucked, or of a column of air when it is blown into, or of the surface of a drum when it is hit. The number of vibrations per second is called

"A" on an 18th-century oboe.

The higher the frequency the higher the pitch. Amplitude variations do not affect pitch.

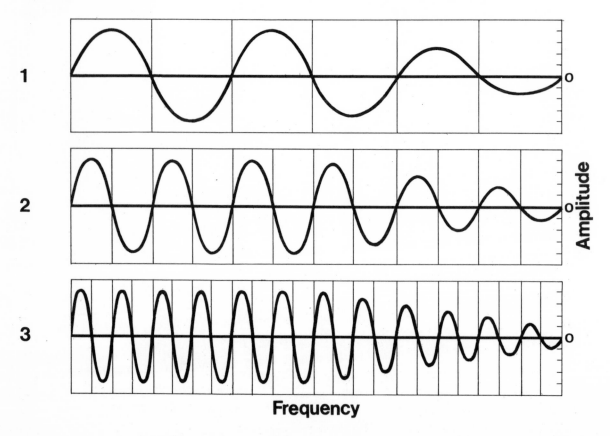

Early demonstrations of acoustics.

the *frequency.* The higher the frequency, the higher the note will be. The lowest note on the piano is about 30, the highest is about 4000. Doubling the frequency of a note produces the note an octave higher. Letter-names are written in the following way to describe each level of pitch:

Middle C=*c'*

1 octave above=*c''* 1 octave below=*c*
2 octaves above=*c'''* 2 octaves below=*C*
3 octaves above=*c''''* 3 octaves below=*C,*

In acoustics, a note has three characteristics: pitch, loudness, and quality. Loudness depends on the amount of energy used to produce the vibration: this can be measured by the *amplitude* of the vibration, which is the distance that a vibrating surface moves from its position of rest. The greater the amount of energy, the louder the sound will be. Loudness is measured in *decibels.* The sounds used in music can vary from about 25 decibels to about 100 decibels. The quality of a note is what makes us able to recognize the characteristic sound of the different instruments, even when we cannot see the players. It is the result of *harmonics,* which are caused by the fact that a vibrating body, such as a string, vibrates simultaneously as a whole and in sections of one half, one third, one fourth, etc. The frequency of the vibration of the whole length of the string produces the *fundamental,* which is the note itself. The frequencies of the harmonics are exact multiples of the frequency of the fundamental. The harmonics have the ratios 2:3:4:5:6: etc. If the fundamental is *C*

The "white-note" octave from A to A.
Below, four octaves of the C to C scale.

A B C D E F G A

MIDDLE C

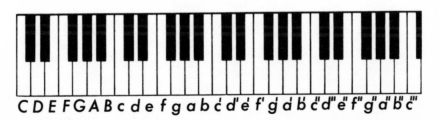

C D E F G A B c d e f g a b c' d' e' f' g' a' b' c'' d'' e'' f'' g'' a'' b'''

(frequency 65), the second harmonic will be *c* (130), the third will be *g* (195), the fourth *c'* (260), the fifth *e'* (325), the sixth *g'* (390), etc. This is known as the *harmonic series*. These faint harmonics cannot be heard distinctly because their amplitude is so much less than that of the fundamental.

AIR A tune or melody. The notes in a tune, like the words in a sentence, have to be put in an order that will convey something to the listener. A tune often consists of short phrases linked together like the phrases between the commas in a sentence of words. Musical phrases are very often balanced, like the lines in a verse of poetry, and sometimes they are repeated; this makes the shape of the tune easy to memorize. An air is called a *theme* when it is developed into a longer piece of music.

BEAT A "beat" is the name given to the pulse that we feel when we are singing or playing or listening to music. When a conductor is "beating time" he is indicating the *pulse* of the music. Beats can be quick or slow according to the speed, or *tempo*, of the music. Tunes can have a variety of quick and slow notes while keeping to the same regular pulse. These various lengths of notes are called *note-values*. The notes in the diagram show a *whole note*, or *semibreve*; 2 *half notes*, or *minims*; 4 *quarter notes*, or *crotchets*; 8 *eighth notes*, or *quavers*; 16 *sixteenth notes*, or *semiquavers*; 32 *thirty-second notes*, or *demisemiquavers*. Each of these note-values has its equivalent length of silence, called a *rest*.

C CLEF, F CLEF, AND G CLEF In written music, which is called *notation*, the *clef* is the clue to the pitch of a note. The diagram shows the three signs used as clefs. In order to be able to indicate the other notes above or below these clefs, musicians use five parallel horizontal lines called the *stave* or *staff*. Notes are written on the lines and the spaces between the lines. When notes are too high or too low to be placed on the stave, short extra lines, called *leger lines*, are used. (See the diagram at the bottom of p. 69.)

Although the lines of the stave are equidistant, the distance in sound from one note to the next

Well may the KEEL ROW

The air called The Keel Row.

Note values related to the whole note.

Note values and their equivalent rests.

The G clef, C clef, and F clef.

68

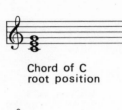

Chord of C
root position

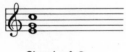

Chord of C
first inversion

Broken chord of C

The C chord.

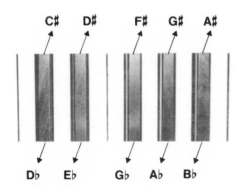

Chromatic notes.

Four octaves of the C to C scale. (See the pitch diagram on p. 67).

is not always the same. In the ladder of sound, or *scale*, from C to C the distance between B and C, and between E and F, is only half the size of all the other steps. Whole steps are called *tones*; half-sized steps are *semitones*. Each step, or *degree*, of a scale can be numbered 1, 2, 3, 4, 5, 6, 7 in relation to the first note.

CHORD Every note has its "own" chord, consisting of the note itself, the third note above it, and the fifth note above it. These three-note chords are called *triads*. C-E-G is the triad of C. It is in the *root position* because the note that the chord belongs to is in the bass. Chords need not be played "solid," with each note sounding simultaneously: the notes can be played one after another, as a *broken chord*. When the notes of a broken chord are repeated at a higher or lower octave, they become an *arpeggio*.

CHROMATIC NOTES If you play Middle C on the piano and move up to the octave C above it, using each "black" note as well as each "white" note in turn, you will have mounted a ladder of 12 equidistant steps, each step being a semitone in size. This is the *chromatic scale* on C. The "black" note a semitone above C is called C *sharp*. The note a semitone above D is D sharp, and in the same way the notes a semitone above F, G, and A are F sharp, G sharp, and A sharp. The five "black" notes in the chromatic scale on C are called by quite different names if they are thought of as the semitone *below* a "white" note instead of above it. For instance, the "black" note a semitone below B is B *flat*. In the same way, the notes a semitone below A, G, E, and D are A flat, G flat, E flat, and D flat.

COUNTING In the early stages of learning to play a piece of music it is helpful to count the beats in order to keep time. A composer can choose any note-value as the unit for counting. And he can choose to count in two, three, four, five, six,

seven, or any number of units. The vertical strokes that help the eye to measure the music in two, three, four, etc., units are *bar-lines*. The "distance in time," or duration, between one bar-line and the next is called a *bar* or a *measure*. There is no need for the composer to write 1, 2, etc., over the units in every bar; instead, he just writes a *time-signature* at the beginning of his music. The lower number represents the unit of time according to its value in terms of a whole note. The number on the top of a time-signature shows how many units there are to the bar. Note-values of different lengths can be grouped in *time-patterns*. The two vertical lines at the end of the examples on this page are called a *double bar*, which is short for "double barline." A double bar is always used at the end of a piece of music, or at the end of a section. A double bar with dots to one side of it shows that a section is to be *repeated* (see The Keel Row, p. 68).

If a time-pattern in 3/4 needs a note lasting throughout the three beats of the bar, a *dot* is placed after a minim to add an extra beat to its length. *Dotted notes* can be used with any time-signature, whenever any note-value has to last for one and a half times its normal length. In the last bar of the 5/4 example on this page there is no single note-value equal to five crotchets, so a curved line called a *tie* is used to join two notes.

DOH   The modern equivalent of Ut (see page 16). Each scale degree has its special name. For instance, in the system known as *tonic sol-fa*, the seven notes of the ascending scale of C can

A conductor beating time.

Time signatures and patterns.

Dotted notes are like tied notes.

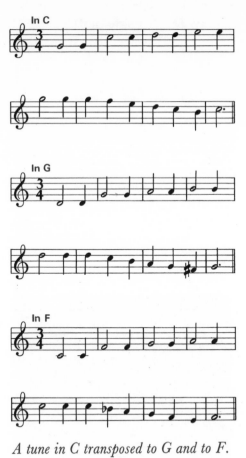

A tune in C transposed to G and to F.

A bagpipe player.

be called *doh*, *ray*, *me*, *fah*, *soh*, *lah*, and *te*. An alternative way of naming these notes is to call them *tonic*, *supertonic*, *mediant*, *sub-dominant*, *dominant*, *sub-mediant*, *leading-note*. These special names can be a help in *transposition*, when a tune has to be transposed to a different level of pitch, while keeping its tones and semitones in the same relative position.

DRONE A long sustained note that goes on and on while other, shorter notes move up and down above it. (The name comes from the drone of the bagpipes.) This is one of the easiest ways of learning to recognize an *interval*, which is the combined sound of two notes played at the same time. If you play the scale of C on the piano with the first note held as a drone, the result will be intervals of a *unison*, *second*, *third*, *fourth*, *fifth*, *sixth*, *seventh*, and *octave*. The size of some of the intervals, measured in tones and semitones, varies according to the position of the semitones in the scale: larger intervals are *major*, smaller are *minor*. Nearly all the "white" note fourths and fifths are described as "perfect": the exceptions are the fourth from F up to B, which is called *augmented*, and the fifth from B up to F which is called *diminished*. Some intervals are described as *consonant*; others are described as *dissonant*. *Perfect consonances* are unisons, octaves, perfect fifths and perfect fourths; *imperfect consonances* are major thirds, minor thirds, major sixths, and minor sixths; and *dissonances* are major and minor seconds, major and minor sevenths, and all augmented and diminished intervals.

The size of the intervals varies according to where the semitones occur.

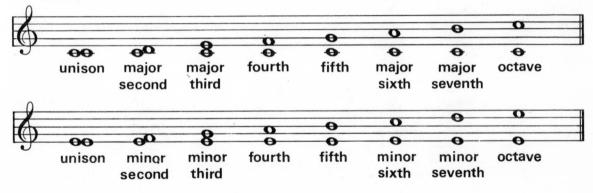

DYNAMICS The gradation of loudness and softness in music. Musicians do not reckon in decibels when they are singing or playing; they think of "loud" or "soft" as relative, using the Italian word *forte*, written *f*, for loud, and *piano*, written *p*, for soft. Other dynamics are shown in the diagram on this page.

ENSEMBLE Music for a group of performers. An *instrumental ensemble* may be a *duo* (duet), *trio*, *quartet*, *quintet*, *sextet*, etc., but it is seldom for more than twelve players, because in a larger group it would be necessary to have a conductor. Music played by a small group without a conductor is called *chamber music*, because it was not originally intended to be heard in a vast concert hall.

A *vocal ensemble* is a small group of soloists working together. The part-songs they sing may be for men's voices, or for women's voices, but they are usually for mixed voices, or S.A.T.B., which means *soprano, alto, tenor, bass*.

EXPRESSION Every piece of music has its own character. In a song, the words will immediately tell the singer what the mood should be. But in instrumental music the brief instructions "quick"

*m**p*** = Fairly soft

*p**p*** = Very soft

*m**f*** = Fairly loud

ff = Very loud

Getting louder

Getting softer

An instrumental ensemble—a quintet.

A vocal ensemble.

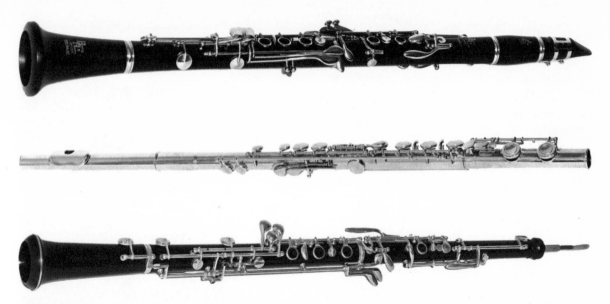

Woodwind Instruments *Above, from top to bottom, a clarinet, a flute, and an oboe. Below, a band of oboes and bassoons playing at the coronation of Louis XV of France in 1715.*

or "slow," "loud" or "soft" may not tell the player enough, and the composer will have to add some more detailed directions called *expression marks*. These are nearly always written in Italian.

A phrase that is to be sung or played very smoothly can be written with a curved line, called a *slur*, linking its notes together. Slurs are *phrase marks*. Phrasing in music is like phrasing in acting. In a scene on the stage, each phrase has to be spoken so that it conveys its dramatic meaning to the audience. In a piece of music, each phrase has to be sung or played so that it conveys its musical meaning to the listener.

FAMILIES OF INSTRUMENTS

1. WOODWIND   The *flute* is a cylindrical tube with the upper end closed. It is held crosswise and the player blows across the mouth-hole and makes his breath strike the edge of it in order to set in vibration the column of air in the tube. The other holes are finger-holes, which can be covered or uncovered to produce any note that is needed. Each different fingering alters the length of the vibrating air column, and this alters the pitch of the note. Modern flutes have metal levers called keys to cover the holes; the connecting mechanism makes it easier to play difficult changes of fingering swiftly and smoothly. The range, or *compass*, of the flute is from *c'* (or *b* flat) to about *a'''*. In the lowest octave the notes are gentle: they become clearer and more penetrating the higher they go. There is a smaller version of the flute, called the *piccolo*: the sound of its compass is from *d''* to about *a''''*, but the notes are written an octave lower than they sound, to avoid too many leger lines.

The *oboe* is a conical pipe with double reed fixed to the upper end. The player puts this double reed to his lips and allows a very little of his breath to pass into the slight opening between the two reeds, so that they begin vibrating against each other. The oboe has a compass from *b* flat to about *d'''* or *e'''*. Its tone is beautifully expressive in the middle range, but the highest notes are thin. There is an alto oboe called the *english horn*, or *cor anglais*. Its compass is from *e* flat to about *g''*. The bass member of the oboe family is called the *bassoon* (in Italian, *fagotto*). It is so large that it has to be

Expression Marks

Accelerando: getting quicker
Adagio : slow and leisurely
Agitato : agitated
Allargando: broadening out
Allegro: quick and cheerful
Andante: gently moving
Animato: animated
Calando: gradually softer and slower
Cantabile : singing tone
Dolce : sweetly
Energico : energetic
Espressivo : expressive
Giocoso : gaily
Grave : slow and solemn
Grazioso: gracefully
Largamente: broadly
Largo : slow and stately
Legato : smoothly
Leggiero : lightly
Lento doloroso: slowly and sadly
Maestoso : majestically
Marcato : marked
Moderato : at a moderate pace
Morendo : dying away
Pesante : heavily
Presto : very quick
Rallentando : slowing down
Risoluto : boldly
Ritardando: getting slower
Rubato : not too strictly
Semplice : simply
Sostenuto : sustained
Staccato : brought off short
Stringendo : gradually faster
Tranquillo : calm
Vivace: quick and lively

Finger positions for the recorder.

Trumpeters in an orchestra.

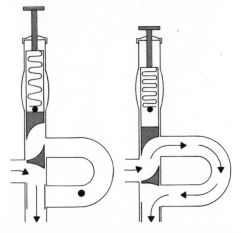

A brass valve closed and open.

held diagonally, with an extra length of tube to connect the mouthpiece to the player's lips. The bassoon's compass is from *B*, flat to about *c''*.

The *clarinet* is a cylindrical pipe. The mouthpiece is beak-shaped on the upper side to allow the player to hold it between his lips; the underside is flat and slotted, with a single reed fixed to it. When the player lets his breath enter the instrument, the reed vibrates against the slot. The compass is *e* to about *e'''*. The lowest notes can sound hollow and mysterious and the high notes can sound like distant trumpets.

2. BRASS All brass instruments consist of a long brass tube and a cupped mouthpiece. They are "lip-vibrated," which means that the player's lips provide the equivalent of reeds. The long tube of the modern *horn* is wound round and round. The open notes of the horn are the notes of the harmonic series. In the 19th century, instrument makers added *valves*—short pieces of tube that could temporarily lower the pitch of any open note without altering its dynamics. This made it possible for horn players to achieve a chromatic scale of three and a half octaves. The horn can be made to sound fierce, but it also has a mellow, singing tone which can blend well with woodwind instruments.

The *trumpet* is a higher-sounding instrument than the horn, and its shape gives it a more brilliant character. The compass is from *f* sharp to about *a''*.

The *trombone*, like all brass instruments, has the open notes of the harmonic series, but long before valves were invented it could produce the remaining notes with the help of a separate U-shaped piece of tube called a *slide*. This can be slid forward or backward while playing. Each change of position increases the "speaking length" of the instrument, which lowers the pitch of the harmonic series by a semitone. The player can therefore produce a chromatic scale of two and a half octaves. The compass of the *tenor trombone* is from *E* to *b'* flat. The *bass trombone* has a compass a fourth lower.

The *bass tuba* can play lower notes than the bass trombone. In character it is mellower than the trombone, and much more like a horn. It is a valved instrument, with a compass from *D*, to *a'* flat.

3. STRINGED INSTRUMENTS (Bowed) The *violin* is the most important member of this family. It has four open strings tuned to *g d' a' e''*. When the player puts a finger on a string he shortens its vibrating length, which raises the pitch of the open note. In this way he can produce a chromatic scale with a compass from G sharp to higher than the human ear can hear. The viola is a larger instrument than the violin: its four strings are tuned to *c g d' a'*. The lowest octave can produce a warm, rich sound. The part is written in the alto clef, with the treble clef for the high notes, which can go up to about *c'''*. The *cello* is so much larger than the viola that it has to be held downward. The cello's four strings are tuned *C G d a*. The part is written in the bass clef, with the tenor clef for fairly high notes, and the treble clef for very high notes, which can go up to *g''*, or even higher. The *double bass* (in Italian, *contra-basso*) is so large that the player has to sit on a high stool in order to hold it. As the stopped notes are so far apart, the strings are tuned in fourths, to *E, A, D G*. The part is written in the bass clef an octave higher than it sounds. The tenor clef is used for high notes, but the double bass is not effective in its highest register, except in the ethereal harmonics that all stringed instruments can produce by touching a string very lightly at the appropriate places for producing the harmonic series.

All the members of the violin family can produce short, somewhat dry notes without using the bow, by plucking the strings with a finger or thumb. *Pizzicato* is the word for plucking. The word *arco* after a *pizzicato* passage shows that the bow is to be used again.

4. STRINGED INSTRUMENTS (Plucked) The modern *harp* has a string for each note of the diatonic C to C scale throughout six and a half octaves. It has seven pedals; each pedal controls one of the seven notes at every octave. The strings are tuned to the notes a semitone below the scale of C; with a single movement of the foot all the C flats are raised to the natural C, and at a second movement they are raised another semitone to C sharp. In this way it is possible for the player to produce any note from *C,* flat to *g''''* flat. Other modern stringed instruments that

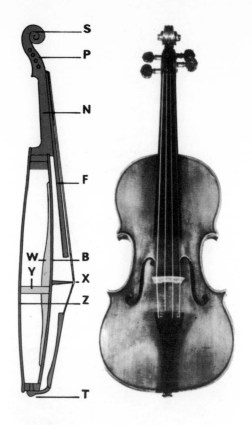

The parts of the violin.
S=Scroll, P=pegs, N=neck,
F=fingerboard, W=base bar,
Y=soundpost, B=table, X=bridge,
Z=back, T=tail piece

Early plucked stringed instruments.

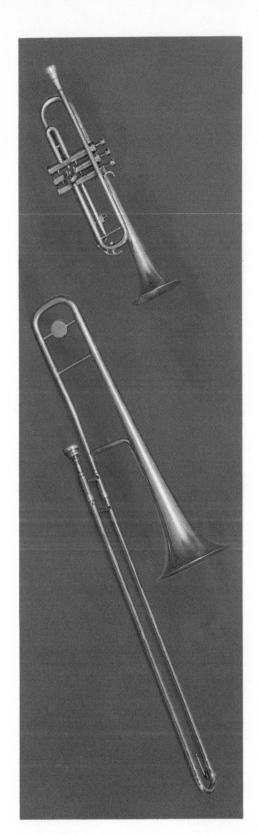
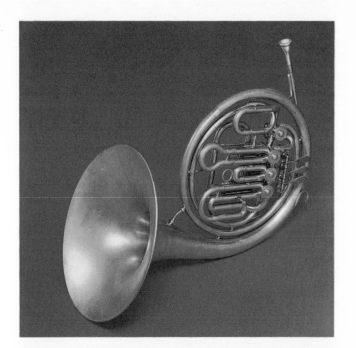

Brass Instruments *Trumpet (top left), trombone (bottom left), horn (top right), and bass tuba (bottom right).*

are plucked are members of the lute and guitar families. The *lute* is an instrument with a body shaped like half a pear, a flat neck with seven or more frets, and a peg-box bent back at an angle. It is a quiet, expressive instrument with a varying number of strings tuned in fourths and thirds. The *guitar* has a body with a flat back, and sides that curve inward. The modern guitar has six strings, tuned to $E\ A\ d\ g\ b\ e'$. The lute and guitar are related to many other instruments, including the *mandolin*, the *zither*, and the *banjo*.

5. KEYBOARD INSTRUMENTS The *organ* is a wind instrument played by means of a keyboard. Modern organs are electrically blown. The picture on page 38 shows the keyboards, called manuals, the pedalboard, and the many knobs, called stops, that control the hundreds of pipes.

The *piano*, or *pianoforte*, is a stringed instrument played by means of a keyboard. When the player puts his fingers down on the keys, the strings are struck by felt-covered hammers, which are connected by an elaborate mechanism called the *action*.

6. PERCUSSION INSTRUMENTS The most important of the percussion instruments with definite pitch is the set of *timpani*, or *kettledrums*. (A single kettledrum is seldom used.) The calfskin "head," stretched across the copper "shell," can be

A lute player.

An early organ with hand bellows. Below, the action of a piano.

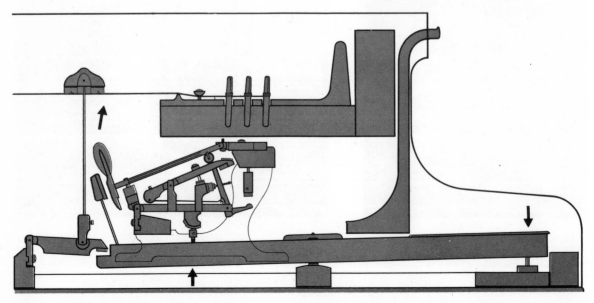

Some early percussion instruments.

A modern percussion player.

tightened or loosened to produce notes of a higher or lower pitch. Timpani are played with two felt-ended wooden sticks, which can hit single notes in any time-pattern the composer wants, or can play a continuous roll, or tremolo, on one note, varying the dynamics from *ppp* up to *fff*. Recently a mechanical device has been invented for altering the pitch of a drum by a controlling pedal; these *chromatic timpani* are now used for music needing rapid changes of tuning. Other percussion instruments with definite pitch include the *glockenspiel*, an instrument like a primitive keyboard: its horizontal steel plates, arranged in varying lengths from long up to short, are played with a hammer in each hand. The *xylophone* is like a wooden glockenspiel. *Tubular bells* are metal tubes suspended from a frame and struck with a hammer. They can be used to imitate the sound of church bells. The *celesta*, which looks like a very small upright piano, is a kind of "keyboard glockenspiel": its notes are produced by steel bars of different lengths, which are struck by hammers connected to a short keyboard by a simplified piano action.

The most important of the percussion instruments of indefinite pitch is the *side drum*, a small cylindrical drum with two heads stretched over a metal shell. The upper head is the "batter head," which the player strikes with his two wooden drumsticks. The lower head, or "snare-head," has two strings called snares stretched tightly across it. The *bass drum* is very much thicker and slacker, and it is played with a large felt-headed stick. The *tambourine* is a small drum with a single vellum head. It has circular metal disks called "jingles" loosely inserted round the frame. It can be struck on the vellum with the fingers, knuckles, palm of the hand, or on the knee, according to the dynamics needed; or it can be shaken rapidly to produce a *tremolo*. The *triangle* is made of steel, with one angle left open: it is struck with a small steel beater. The *cymbals* are two circular brass plates, held by leather straps. They are played either by clashing one against the other or by suspending one and touching it with a timpani stick. The *gong* is a large circular disk of metal, which is struck almost in the center with a heavy soft-headed beater.

FUGUE The word "fugal," from the Latin for "chasing after," or "putting to flight," refers to the way in which a musical phrase can be imitated by a second voice or instrument coming in a little later with the same phrase. The word *canon* is used to describe music, either vocal or instrumental, where the imitation follows the notes of the tune quite strictly to the very end. The entries in imitation can be at a different level of pitch. In elaborate canons there may be entries of the tune in *augmentation*, with slower note-values, or in *diminution*, with quicker note-values. The tune may be *inverted* by turning its melodic intervals upside-down, or it may *retrograde*—going backwards—with the last note first and the first note last. These devices are used not only in a strict canon but also in a *fugue*, where the instruments or voices, having entered in imitation, are free to continue with different phrases.

GROUND (In Italian, *basso ostinato*) The notes of a short bass part repeated over and over again to form the foundation of a whole piece of music.

HARMONY Learning harmony means learning to move from one chord to the next so that the journey sounds purposeful and there is a feeling of home-coming at the end. Since triads are built up from the bass note, it is necessary to listen to the way one bass note follows another and to recognize whether the bass note is the root of the chord or not. The *dominant chord* moving to the *tonic chord* is described as a *perfect cadence*, or full close. The tonic to the dominant is an *imperfect cadence*: it is a half close, like a semicolon. The word "harmony" is sometimes used to describe chordal music, such as a hymn, in contrast with contrapuntal music, such as a fugue or a canon. But harmony and counterpoint are continually overlapping: there is no fixed boundary between them. In its widest musical sense, the word "harmony" cannot be defined in a glossary: it is connected with the Greek meaning of "proportion," where everything has to be joined so that it fits together.

KEY If the white-notes scale of C to C is transposed to the level of G to G with an F sharp for the leading note, it becomes the *major scale* of

Manuscripts in Bach's handwriting of (top) fugal music, (center) a ground bass, (bottom) chordal music.

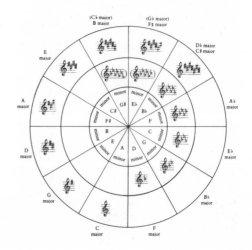

Key relationships.

The scale of G major and the key signature of G major.

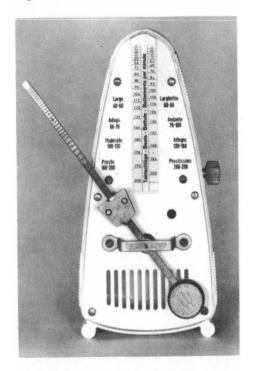

Two modern metronomes.

G. Tunes that are founded on the notes of the scale of G major are described as in the *key* of G major. A *key signature* is written immediately after the clef at the beginning of each new line of music. An F sharp in a key signature shows that every F, at whatever octave it occurs, must be sharpened. G major is the first of the *sharp keys*. The order of the sharp keys goes up in fifths. When the scale of C major is transposed to F, with B flat for the subdominant, it becomes the scale of F major, with one flat in its key signature. The order of the *flat keys* goes *down* in fifths. Every major key has its *relative minor*, which shares the same key signature. The order of the keys and their relationship can be seen in the diagram on the opposite page.

METRONOME A measured pendulum for indicating the exact speed of a piece of music. It consists of a rod with a weight at both ends. The swinging rod can be set in motion either by a touch of the hand or by clockwork. The weight at the upper end is movable, and can be adjusted to any of the figures, ranging from 40 to about 200, which represent the number of units of time in the duration of a whole minute. Metronome marks are useful for suggesting the pulse of the music before beginning to sing or play, but musicians would never keep the machine ticking away throughout the whole piece of music, because a rhythmical pulse is not rigid like clockwork.

MICROTONES The very small changes of pitch that exist between the twelve notes of the chromatic scale. They can be heard when a string player slides his finger slowly up and down the distance of an octave instead of fingering each separate note. The fixed level of pitch for the twelve equal divisions of the octave, which is known as *equal temperament*, has only been in use during the past two hundred years; it enables musicians to play in any key and to change from one key to another.

MODULATION Moving from one key to another. In a true modulation, several bars are needed to establish the fact that the music has entered a new key and means to stay there for a while: it is a process connected with musical form. (See MUSICAL FORMS.)

MOTION In a single line of melody, a phrase that moves stepwise up or down is in *conjunct motion* and a phrase with "leaps" of melodic intervals larger than a second is in *disjunct motion*. In contrapuntal music, two voices moving up and down while keeping the same distance apart are in *parallel motion*. Two voices moving in opposite directions are in *contrary motion*. When one voice moves up or down and the other remains at its original level of pitch, the two voices are in *oblique motion*.

MUSICAL FORMS, TEXTURES AND STYLES *Form* in music is the sense of wholeness that the composer has in his mind, and that the listener can recognize, to the best of his ability, when the piece has been sung or played from beginning to end. Musical *forms* are the shapes and structures that a composer uses. In a short tune it is easy to hear the balance of the phrases. In music that is more elaborate it is difficult to talk about the form without also mentioning the texture. For instance, in *Variations on a Theme* the first variation may be in blocks of chords like a hymn—a texture called *homophonic*, or "alike-sounding." The second variation may be a fugue—a texture called *polyphonic* or "many-sounding." Forms and textures change with the changing styles of each century. Historians refer to various main periods during the last thousand years or so, giving approximate dates for each period.

Before 850. Early Middle Ages. *Plainsong*: a single line of melody, sung with unmeasured rhythm.

850-1200. Later Middle Ages. The beginnings of polyphony: two or more voices chanting in parallel fourths or fifths (9th and 10th centuries), in contrary motion (11th century), in long flowing lines over held notes in augmentation (12th century), and (in the late 12th century) in measured rhythm with a regular pulse and time-patterns.

1200-1300. *Ars antiqua*, "the ancient art." *Motets*, which were unaccompanied choral settings of a Latin text from the church service. Secular music was sung by troubadours in France and by minnesingers in Germany.

1300-1450. *Ars nova*, "the new art." *Canons* and *rounds*, such as "Sumer is icumen in,"

Monks chanting.

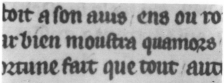

Medieval instrumentalists.

14th-century musicians in Germany.

Bowed Stringed Instruments   *The violin family: top left, violin; top center, viola; bottom left, cello or violoncello; right, double bass.*

(anon. c. 1310). In motets, the counterpoint was usually for three voices, and was sometimes with instrumental accompaniment.

1450-1550. Early Renaissance. The Church music included settings of the Mass (*Kyrie, Gloria, Credo, Sanctus* and *Benedictus, Agnus Dei*) for four or more voices, with contrapuntal entries in imitation.

1550-1620. "Golden age" Renaissance. Masses and motets for many voices. Secular vocal music included *madrigals* "in the mother tongue," and lutenist songs for solo voice with lute accompaniment. Instrumental music was often fugal: the forms included the *canzona* or *canzon da sonar*, "a song for sounding"; the *ricercar* with entries in close imitation, (the name means "to search out"); and the *fantazia*. These instrumental works were either for a *whole consort* of instruments of the same family, or for a broken consort of instruments from different families. Renaissance dance forms included the stately *Pavane*, the more cheerful *Galliard*, the *Coranto* with its quick running figures, and the *Jig* with its lively skipping rhythm.

The earliest experiments in *opera* were made in Italy at the end of the Renaissance; the poetic script, or *libretto*, was set to a kind of musical speech called *recitative*, which was accompanied on the harpsichord.

1620-1700. Early Baroque. Composers of early Baroque opera introduced songs called *arias* between their recitatives. They also wrote choruses that were accompanied by an instrumental ensemble called an *orchestra*, directed from the harpsichord. The orchestra provided an overture, and incidental dances that included the graceful *Sarabande* and the *Minuet*. Other instrumental forms included *Variations on a Theme*, and the Baroque *Sonata*. The word "sonata" means "sound-piece." There were two different kinds of sonata: the *sonata da camera*, or chamber sonata, consisting of several dances such as the *Allemande, Courante, Sarabande*, and *Gigue*; and the *sonata da chiesa*, or church sonata, which had four sections, or *movements*, called by the Italian words describing their different speeds: for example, *Adagio, Allegro, Largo, Vivace*.

1700-1750. Late Baroque. Early 18th-century opera needed a style of singing called *bel canto*

Early opera in Italy.

Baroque music-making.

An 18th-century duo.

84

Chamber music in the home.

An 18th-century minuet.

A 19th-century waltz.

in which beauty of sound was more important than dramatic expression. There was more opportunity for dramatic choruses in an oratorio—an extended work, usually with a sacred libretto, intended for concert performance. The Baroque *cantata* was written for performance during a church service. The choruses were usually founded on a hymn-tune, or *chorale*. Recitatives linked the arias, which often had an additional tune for a solo instrument, called *obligato* (or *obbligato*). (See also the reference to Passion music on p. 39.)

The 18th-century equivalent of the *sonata da camera* was the *Suite*, or *Partita*, a short collection of contrasting dance tunes in the same key. Suites were sometimes written for the orchestra, which was still a fairly small ensemble directed from the harpsichord.

1750-1820. The Classical Period. *Sonata form* refers to the structure of the first movement of a classical sonata: first subject, in the tonic; bridge passage; second subject, in the dominant; development section leading to the recapitulation, when the first subject returns in its own key. Other movements in a classical sonata could be a *Theme and Variations*, (but not on a *Ground*), or a movement in the form of an aria, or a *Minuet and Trio*. The last movement of a sonata was often a quick *Rondo*, with the first section repeated after each new section.

The form of the sonata was the basis of all classical instrumental music, including the *string* quartet and the orchestral *symphony* and *concerto*, which were no longer directed from the harpsichord. It also influenced the structure of opera and oratorio.

1820-1900. The Romantic Period. New forms in 19th-century music include the *lied*—a song with equal partnership for singer and pianist, and the *song cycle*—a collection of separate songs linked together to make one complete work. Soon after 1800 the classical Minuet went out of fashion, and the Waltz was the most popular dance throughout the century. The development of the piano encouraged composers to write solos that were often "character pieces." Sonatas and symphonies followed the outline of the classical structure, but were much more passionate in style. Descriptive works for orchestra were called *symphonic poems* or *tone poems*.

Orchestras became very much larger, and the invention of valves for brass instruments, enabling them to play chromatic scales, altered the texture and dynamics of orchestral music and operatic accompaniment. Opera composers in Italy continued to give their soloists arias to sing, but in Germany the invention of Wagnerian "Music Drama" broke away from the earlier traditions influencing many late-19th-century composers, and caused various reactions at the beginning of our own century. (For 20th-century changes in form, texture, and style, see TONALITY AND ATONALITY.)

ORCHESTRA AND ORCHESTRATION The word "orchestra" was first used in about 1600, when opera was invented: it is Greek for "dancing-place"—the space between the stage and the auditorium that we now call the "orchestra pit." The 17th-century orchestra was a small ensemble directed from the harpsichord. It was not until after 1750 that the harpsichord was banished and the orchestra was directed by the principal first violinist, who was called the *leader*. The normal classical orchestra consisted of two flutes, two oboes, two clarinets, two bassoons, two horns, two trumpets, two timpani, and strings: first violins, second violins, violas, cellos, and basses. From the early 19th century onward the director of an orchestra has been a *conductor*, who uses a stick, or baton, instead of an instrument to control the larger number of players. The full orchestra of today is no larger than it was at the end of the 19th century. The four main groups are the woodwind, brass, percussion, and strings. (See FAMILIES OF INSTRUMENTS.) They are written in that order in the *full score*, beginning at the top of the page with the flute or piccolo and going down the page to the double bass. A normal woodwind section can consist of two flutes and piccolo, two oboes and english horn, two clarinets and bass clarinet, and two bassoons and double bassoon. A normal brass section can consist of four horns, playing in pairs (I and III taking the higher notes, and II and IV the lower), two or three trumpets, two tenor trombones, one bass trombone, and tuba. The percussion section can consist of two or three timpani (one player), and side drum, bass drum, gong, cymbals, tambourine, and triangle (divided between

A scene from a Wagner opera.

A modern full orchestra.

Plucked Stringed Instrument   *This concert harp, made in 1870, is almost six feet high. Seven pedals enable each of its 46 strings to be raised in pitch a half or a whole tone.*

two players). If the celesta is needed, the part is written just below the percussion in the full score. The harp part is written below the celesta and, if a piano or organ is needed, the part is written below the harp. The number of string players depends on the balance of wind and percussion in the orchestration: in a large full orchestra the proportion can be 20 first violins, 18 second violins, 14 violas, 12 cellos and 8 double basses. The size of a full orchestra depends on the particular work that is being played. The placing of an orchestra depends on the choice of program, the acoustics of the hall, and the conductor's preference. Some conductors like the cellos on their right: others prefer to place the second violins there; but all agree in having the first violins on their left, the wind behind the strings, and the percussion behind the wind.

ORNAMENTS   The decorations that composers sometimes add to their tunes are call *ornaments* or *grace-notes*. Seventeenth-century singers and players usually improvised their gracing, but later composers have shown what they wanted in writing. Grace-notes are written smaller than ordinary notes.

PENTATONIC SCALE   The word pentatonic can apply to a tune founded on any five notes. In Western music the name is used for "gapped" scales without semitones. Pentatonic traditional tunes can be found in many countries throughout the world: they are a link between Western and "non-Western" music.

RHYTHM   The word "rhythm" comes from the Greek verb "to flow." In music, as in dancing, rhythm is concerned with alternating tension and relaxation: this can be felt in the rise and fall of a single line of melody; in dissonant harmonies moving toward the *resolution* of consonance; and in an *accelerando* and *crescendo* followed by a *rallentando* and *diminuendo*. In measured music, the word "rhythm" is often used to distinguish the time signature: for instance, "a six-eight rhythm." Time-patterns are all-important in the tension and relaxation of a rhythmical phrase, but time-patterns and speeds are only the signposts to rhythm: the true "flow" depends on phrasing. "Unrhythmical" playing or singing

Band music for marching.

Early 18th-century ornaments.

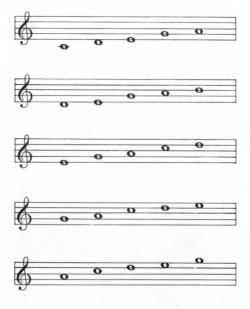

Pentatonic "white-note" scales.

A medieval German church organ.

can be the result of hurrying, through nervousness or through over-emphasis; or it can be the result of dragging, through lack of technique or through sentimentality. Rhythm cannot be learned from a textbook, because music is concerned with feeling as well as with thinking.

TONALITY AND ATONALITY The word tonality means "allegiance to a tonal center." At the beginning of the 20th century there were composers who began to experiment in non-Western scales, or in microtones such as quarter-tones or sixth-tones, or in two keys at once (bitonality), or several keys at once (polytonality). Others experimented in atonality, where no individual note could have power over any other note.

TWELVE-NOTE METHOD OF COMPOSITION The method of composing with "twelve notes related only to one another" dates from the early 1920s; it is founded on the division of the octave into twelve notes a semitone apart, arranged in a fixed order as a *note row* or *series*. The row can be used forward, backward (*retrograde*), upside down (*inverted*), and *retrograde-inverted*; and it can be transposed to any level of pitch.

WIRELESS TRANSMISSION, RECORDING ON TAPE AND DISK, AND ELECTRONIC DEVICES Broadcasting music by radio transmission dates from the early 1920s. The electromagnetic waves that fill the air all around us are intercepted, amplified, and converted into audible sound waves. This has had a revolutionary effect on the lives of professional musicians, since vast numbers of listeners can now hear the same concert without having to leave their homes. The invention of the tape recorder has made it possible for musicians to hear a playback of the sounds they have made during a rehearsal.

Tape recorders are also responsible for *electronic music*, which is a direct result of the mechanical reproduction of sound. Electronically produced sound waves are recorded on tape and then amplified, slowed down, quickened up, reversed, and superimposed until the mixture of combined frequencies produces sounds that have never been heard before. Electronic devices cannot be written in musical notation: the "score" consists of frequency ratios and decibel numbers.

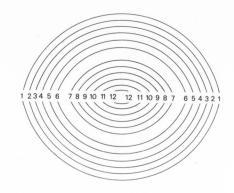
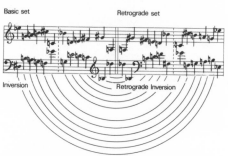

A note row by Arnold Schoenberg.

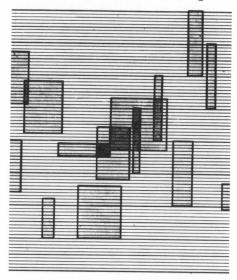

From a "score" for electronic music.

90

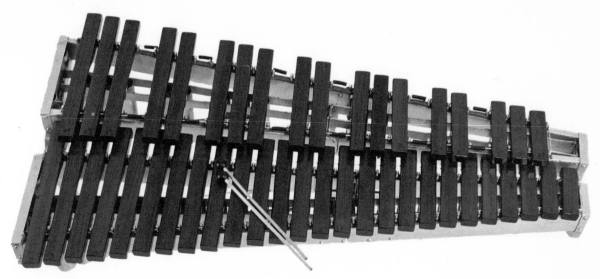

Percussion Instruments *Above, a xylophone. Below, top row from left to right, tubular bells, snare drum, glockenspiel, tenor drum, bass drum; bottom row, pair of pedal timpani, triangle, cymbals, tambourine, and tam-tam gong.*

A Chronological List of Composers

PÉROTIN
French, 12th century

GUILLAUME DE MACHAUT
French, 1300–77

FRANCESCO LANDINO
Italian, *c.* 1325–97

JOHN DUNSTABLE
English, *c.* 1390–1453

GILLES BINCHOIS
Flemish, *c.* 1400–67

GUILLAUME DUFAY
Flemish, *c.* 1400–74

JOHANNES OCKEGHEM
Flemish, *c.* 1430–95

JAKOB OBRECHT
Flemish, *c.* 1430–1505

HEINRICH ISAAC
Flemish, *c.* 1450–1517

JOSQUIN DES PRÉS
Flemish, *c.* 1450–1521

CLEMENT JANEQUIN
French, *c.* 1475–1560

ADRIAN WILLAERT
Flemish, *c.* 1480–1562

JOHN TAVERNER
English, *c.* 1495–1545

CRISTOBAL MORALES
Spanish, *c.* 1500–53

CLAUDE GOUDIMEL
French, *c.* 1505–72

THOMAS TALLIS
English, *c.* 1505–85

ANDREA GABRIELI
Italian, *c.* 1510–86

GIOVANNI PIERLUIGI DA
PALESTRINA,
Italian, 1525–94

ORLANDO LASSUS
Flemish, 1532–94

TOMAS LUIS DE VICTORIA
Spanish, *c.* 1540–1611

WILLIAM BYRD
English, 1543–1623

THOMAS MORLEY
English, 1557–1603

GIOVANNI GABRIELI
Italian, 1557–1612

MELCHIOR VULPIUS
German, *c.* 1560–1615

JAN PIETERSZOON
SWEELINCK
Dutch, 1562–1621

JOHN DOWLAND
English, 1563–1626

CLAUDIO MONTEVERDI
Italian, 1567–1643

MICHAEL PRAETORIUS
German, 1571–1621

JOHN WILBYE
English, 1573–1638

THOMAS WEELKES
English, 1577–1623

ORLANDO GIBBONS
English, 1583–1625

HEINRICH SCHUTZ
German, 1585–1672

JEAN BAPTISTE LULLY
French, 1632–87

DIETRICH BUXTEHUDE
German, 1637–1707

JOHN BLOW
English, 1649–1708

ARCHANGELO CORELLI
Italian, 1653–1713

HENRY PURCELL
English, 1659–95

ALESSANDRO SCARLATTI
Italian, 1660–1725

FRANÇOIS COUPERIN
French, 1668–1733

GEORG PHILIPP TELEMANN
German, 1681–1767

JEAN-PHILIPPE RAMEAU
French, 1683–1764

JOHANN SEBASTIAN BACH
German, 1685–1750

GEORG FRIEDRICH HANDEL
German-English,
1685–1759

DOMENICO SCARLATTI
Italian, 1685–1759

FRANCESCO GEMINIANI
Italian, 1687–1762

THOMAS AUGUSTINE ARNE
English, 1710–78

CHRISTOPH WILLIBALD
GLUCK
Bohemian-German,
1714–87

KARL PHILIPP EMANUEL
BACH
German, 1714–88

FRANZ JOSEPH HAYDN
Austrian, 1732–1809

JOHANN CHRISTIAN BACH
German, 1735–82

WOLFGANG AMADEUS
MOZART
Austrian, 1756–91

SAMUEL WESLEY
English, 1766–1837

LUDWIG VAN BEETHOVEN
German, 1770–1827

CARL MARIA VON WEBER
German, 1786–1826

GIOACCHINO ROSSINI
Italian, 1792–1865

FRANZ SCHUBERT
Austrian, 1797–1828

GAETANO DONIZETTI
Italian, 1797–1848

VINCENZO BELLINI
Italian, 1801–35

HECTOR BERLIOZ
French, 1803–69

MICHAEL GLINKA
Russian, 1804–57

FELIX
MENDELSSOHN-BARTHOLDY
German, 1809–47

FRÉDÉRIC CHOPIN
Polish, 1810–49

ROBERT SCHUMANN
German, 1810–56

FRANZ LISZT
Hungarian, 1811–86

RICHARD WAGNER
German, 1813–83

GUISEPPE VERDI
Italian, 1813–1901

CÉSAR FRANCK
French, 1822–90

BEDŘICH SMETANA
Czech, 1824–84

ANTON BRUCKNER
Austrian, 1824–96

ALEXANDRE BORODIN
Russian, 1833–87

JOHANNES BRAHMS
German, 1833–97

GEORGES BIZET
French, 1838–75

MODEST MOUSSORGSKY
Russian, 1839–81

PETER ILYITCH
TCHAIKOVSKY
Russian, 1840–93

ANTONIN DVOŘÁK
Czech, 1841–1904

EDVARD GRIEG
Norwegian, 1843–1907

NICOLAS RIMSKY-KORSAKOV
Russian, 1844–1908

GABRIEL FAURÉ
French, 1845–1924

EDWARD ELGAR
English, 1857-1934

ISAAC ALBÉNIZ
Spanish, 1860–1909

GUSTAV MAHLER
Austrian, 1860–1911

GLAUDE DEBUSSY
French, 1862–1918

FREDERICK DELIUS
English, 1862–1934

RICHARD STRAUSS
German, 1864–1949

ALEXANDRE GLASUNOV
Russian, 1865–1936

JEAN SIBELIUS
Finnish, 1865–1957

FERRUCIO BUSONI
Italian, 1866–1924

ALEXANDRE SCRIABIN
Russian, 1872–1915

RALPH VAUGHN WILLIAMS
English, 1872–1959

GUSTAV HOLST
English, 1874–1934

ARNOLD SCHOENBERG
Austrian, 1874–1951

MAURICE RAVEL
French, 1875–1937

MANUEL DE FALLA
Spanish, 1876–1946

ERNST VON DOHNANYI
Hungarian, 1877–1960

BÉLA BARTÓK
Hungarian 1881–1945

PERCY GRAINGER
Australian, 1882–1961

ZOLTAN KODALY
Hungarian, 1882–1967

IGOR STRAVINSKY
Russian, b. 1882 – 1972

ANTON WEBERN
Austrian, 1883–1945

ALBAN BERG
Austrian, 1885–1935

SERGE PROKOFIEV
Russian, 1891–1960

DARIUS MILHAUD
French, 1892–1967

PAUL HINDEMITH
German, 1895–1963

GEORGE GERSHWIN
American, 1898–1937

FRANCIS POULENC
French, 1899–1963

AARON COPLAND
American, b. 1900

WILLIAM WALTON
English, b. 1902

LUIGI DALLAPICCOLA
Italian, b. 1904

GOFFREDO PETRASSI
Italian, b. 1904

MICHAEL TIPPETT
English, b. 1905

DMITRI SHOSTAKOVITCH
Russian, b. 1906

OLIVIER MESSIAEN
French, b. 1908

SAMUEL BARBER
American, b. 1910

GIAN-CARLO MENOTTI
American, b. 1911

BENJAMIN BRITTEN
English, b. 1913

LEONARD BERNSTEIN
American, b. 1918

HANS WERNER HENZE
German, b. 1926

Index

Page numbers in *italics* refer to illustration captions.

Picture Credits